GOING TO PAPA AND NANA'S FARM
GINGER'S BIG DAY

BY LOUISE MALECHA

ILLUSTRATED BY KATELYNN ROELIKE

Welcome to the farm!

Ready to see our real farm in action?

We prepared videos for you to
immerse yourself in our dairy farm.
Open your camera and hoover over the QR code below,
click the link that appears and be prepared to
watch, listen, and learn.

I hope you are inspired to learn more about
farm life and to go after one of your dreams.
To learn more about farm life, check out
Malecha Enterprises YouTube channel.

Louise Malecha

Acknowledgements

To Todd Malecha, my husband and biggest supporter.

To Emily Malecha, who was always there to bounce off ideas and collaborate.

To Katelynn Roelike, who brought my story to life with her amazing illustrations, and again has captured life on the farm with her beautiful pictures.

Thank You.

"Ginger's Big Day" is a fun, entertaining, and educational read for farm and nonfarm children alike. Louise Malecha speaks to readers and young listeners with a personal understanding of dairy farm life and through experiences of teaching her own children and grandchildren. Just as Ginger the calf yearns for more milk, you'll want more pages. The book would be great without Augmented Reality, but fortunately, it has that, too.

~ Mike Rankin
Managing editor, Hay & Forage Grower Magazine, W.D. Hoard & Sons Company

Who can resist a curious red calf? *"Ginger's Big Day"* provides a perfect next adventure for Sadie and Jack as they explore Papa and Nana's farm. With its unique read-alone or read-with-help text and vibrant illustrations, this book is sure to be a read-again-and-again favorite!

~ Deb Mercier
Author of the Detective: You series for young readers

"Ginger's Big Day" is a wonderful story. Ginger, an adventurous and spunky red calf, stands out among the herd. As Nana and her grandchildren develop a relationship with Ginger, readers gain a glimpse into life on a real family farm. This fun story also cultivates a sense of responsibility and purpose among school-age readers. This editor and farmer calls it a must-read children's book.

~ Corey Geiger
Managing Editor at Hoard's Dairyman and Author of the books On a Wisconsin Family Farm and The Wisconsin Farm They Built

"Ginger's Big Day" is a fantastic little book about a day in the life of a true farming family. The story is short and sweet, and children will find it relatable and inviting.

~ Peggy McColl
New York Times Best-Selling Author

Louise Malecha's *"Ginger's Big Day"* gives us a glimpse of what it's like on Nana and Papa's farm. The reader learns tasks and words they may not have known before, and Ginger, a quick and curious calf, provides us with some light entertainment. A great read for young ones interested in learning about life on a farm.

~ Nina Kassam
Best-Selling Author of Nope! Not Doing It!

Louise Malecha has done it again! This fun book about life on the farm is as entertaining as it is educational. *"Ginger's Big Day"* takes readers along for an exciting experience, giving young bookworms a glimpse of farm life from a true insider's perspective. Highly recommended!

~ **Judy O'Beirn**
International Best-Selling Author

Published by:
Hasmark Publishing
www.hasmarkpublishing.com

Copyright © 2023 Louise Malecha
First Edition
No part of this book may be reproduced or transmitted in any form or by any means, electronic or mechanical, including photocopying, recording or by any information storage and retrieval system, without written permission from the author, except for the inclusion of brief quotations in a review.

Disclaimer:
This book is designed to provide information and motivation to our readers. It is sold with the understanding that the publisher is not engaged to render any type of psychological, legal, or any other kind of professional advice. The content of each article is the sole expression and opinion of its author, and not necessarily that of the publisher. No warranties or guarantees are expressed or implied by the publisher's choice to include any of the content in this volume. Neither the publisher nor the individual author(s) shall be liable for any physical, psychological, emotional, financial, or commercial damages, including, but not limited to, special, incidental, consequential or other damages. Our views and rights are the same: You are responsible for your own choices, actions, and results.
Permission should be addressed in writing to Louise Malecha at louise@malechaenterprises.com

Editors:
Brad Green (brad@hasmarkpublishing.com)
Deb Mercier (deb.hollmercier@gmail.com)
Layout Artist: Amit Dey (amit@hasmarkpublishing.com)
Illustrator & Cover : Katelynn Roelike

Paperback:
ISBN 13: 978-1-77482-219-7
ISBN 10: 1774822199

Hardcover:
ISBN 13: 978-1-77482-220-3
ISBN 10: 1774822202

To our seven children, who would begin their days feeding calves with me from a young age.

To Ellie, our redheaded granddaughter who enjoys spotting and picking out all the red calves and cows on the farm.

To all our grandchildren, who enjoy seeing the curious little calves every time they have a chance—especially the red ones!

This is Papa and Nana's farm.

This is Papa and Nana with their dog, Spud. Sadie and Jack have come to visit Papa and Nana. Jack brought along Timmy, his turtle.

Papa and Nana have calves on their farm.

The calves live in their own little houses. They have fresh water, food, and a nice, soft bed. Each house has a fence around it. On a farm, a calf's house is called a hutch.

"It is time to feed the calves," says Nana. "Do you want to come with me?"

"Yes, we do!" says Sadie. They jump on the cart beside Spud. "Whoa!" says Jack, as Timmy almost slips out of his hands.

"Jack, you can ride in the milk wagon with Lucy, my helper," says Nana. "Sadie, you will come with me."

Lucy feeds each calf the right amount of milk. Nana and Sadie follow the milk wagon to make sure the calves drink all their milk.

Jack counts the calves, "One, two, three, four..."

"Lucy, there sure are a lot of calves!" says Jack. "Are there always this many?" "Yes, a new calf is born almost every day," says Lucy.

One of the calves is red. Her name is Ginger.

Most of the calves are black and white. Ginger feels special because she is red. Ginger is always curious and full of spunk. She likes to play with her milk and water buckets.

Ginger sees the milk wagon coming. She is hungry!

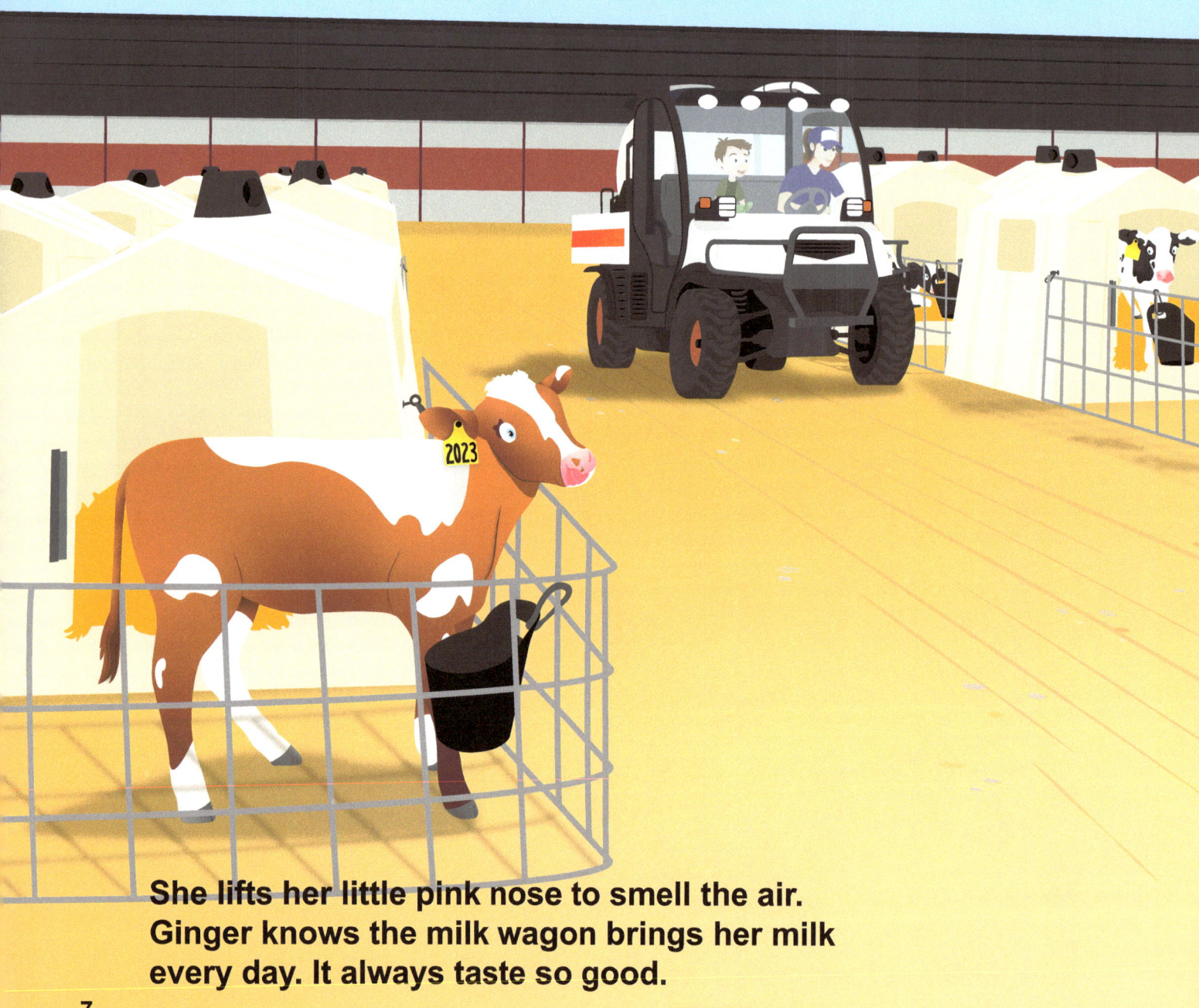

She lifts her little pink nose to smell the air. Ginger knows the milk wagon brings her milk every day. It always taste so good.

Ginger looks for a way to get closer to the milk wagon. She does not want to wait!

Ginger finds a hole. It is just big enough for her. She squeezes between the fence and the hutch.

Ginger is outside of her fence.

Ginger kicks up her heels and jumps in the air. Spud spots her and lets out a bark, "Ruff! Ruff!" He runs after her.

Nana and Sadie hear Spud barking at Ginger.

"Nana, Ginger is running to the milk wagon!" says Sadie. "We better go catch her to take her back to her hutch," says Nana.

Jack sees Ginger trotting to the milk wagon.

"Look, Lucy! Ginger is out and she is coming this way!" says Jack as he holds on tight to Timmy. "What will we do?"

Lucy slows down so Ginger can come by the milk wagon.

"We will let her come to us," says Lucy. "She smells the fresh, warm milk in the milk wagon. When she is close enough, we will be able to catch her!"

Ginger is reaching for Lucy's milk hose.

Ginger tries to get closer and closer to Lucy's milk hose. She sticks out her long, pink tongue to taste the milk.

Nana walks close to Ginger. Lucy jumps off the milk wagon to help Nana.

"Ginger, are you looking for milk?" asks Nana, as she puts her hands around the curious calf. Lucy stands behind her.

Sadie puts out her hand to pet Ginger's red head.

Ginger licks Sadie's fingers. Sadie laughs and says, "It tickles! Oh, now she is sucking on my hand. This calf must be hungry. I like her so much. She is so red and pretty."

Jack jumps off the milk wagon to pet Ginger, too. He holds on tight to Timmy.

Ginger licks Jack's face. "Oh! Oh! Her tongue is rough," says Jack. Timmy gets scared. He pulls his head and feet inside his shell.

Nana leads Ginger back to her hutch. Sadie walks ahead to open the fence.

Spud sniffs the ground after them. Lucy drives the milk wagon to bring Ginger her milk.

Sadie sees the hole in the fence.

"Nana, look!" says Sadie. "I see where Ginger snuck out of the fence." Nana brings Ginger into her pen. There is a bolt and nut missing. "We will have to fix that," says Nana.

Nana asks Lucy to look in the toolbox. The toolbox is on the milk wagon.

Lucy finds a bolt and nut to fix the hole. She helps Nana fix the fence. Now Ginger will be safe in her home.

Lucy fills Ginger's bucket with milk.

Lucy gives Ginger the right amount of milk. Too much milk will give the curious calf a tummy ache.

Ginger drinks up all the milk and moves her bucket around.

"I know Ginger is feeling good when she licks the bottom of the bucket clean," says Nana.

"Ginger looks happy now! Does she have a full tummy?" asks Sadie.

"Calves are like babies and need the right kind of food to grow big and strong," says Nana.

Ginger sniffs and walks in circles to fluff up her soft, straw bed.

"Is Ginger going to sleep?" asks Jack. "Yes, most calves will lay down after they drink their milk," says Nana. "Calves need dry beds to keep them warm and cozy."

"I am so glad Ginger is safe in her little hutch," says Sadie. "Look, Timmy has come out of his shell, again."

"I am glad, too," says Nana. "Ginger did have a very big day! It is nice to see Timmy is not scared anymore. That must mean he is ready for our next adventure!"

Also enjoy these books by Louise Malecha
"Going to Papa and Nana's Farm"
"Going to Papa and Nana's Farm" Activity Book

You can find these on:
Amazon.com
Barnes and Noble.com
Porchlight.com
Indiebound.com

For more information, please visit:
www.louisemalecha.com
Instagram: Louise Malecha
Facebook: Louise Malecha
louise@malechaenterprises.com

For more information about the Malechas' businesses please visit:
www.malechaenterprises.com
Malecha Enterprises YouTube Channel
Instagram: Malecha Enterprises
Facebook: Malecha Enterprises

About the Author and Illustrator

Louise Malecha is an international best-selling author. She is an agriculture woman by heart and loves the farm life. With her husband, Todd, they have built their agriculture business into what it is today, Malecha Enterprises. The Malechas were Farm Journal's Top Producer of 2022. By homeschooling their seven children, she has not only taught them from books, but also from life learning experiences on the farm. She is "Nana" to her grandchildren, who she loves spending time with. She loves brightening her grandchildren's imagination by showing and teaching them activities on their farming operation as she did her own children. If she isn't teaching and mentoring about farm life, you will see her staying active in health and fitness.

Katelynn Roelike is the daughter of Louise Malecha. Katelynn grew up on the farm with her six siblings. Growing up, one of her main responsibilities was to tend to and take care of the calves with her siblings, which taught her responsibility, teamwork, and hard work. Katelynn continues to be a part of the family operation, doing anything from creating and managing the operation's social media accounts to driving a piece of equipment to illustrating her mother's books. Photography, graphic design, and agriculture are some of her strong passions.

www.ingramcontent.com/pod-product-compliance
Lightning Source LLC
LaVergne TN
LVHW071032070426
835507LV00003B/131